Courage and Conviction

Ethical Dilemmas, Decision-Making, and Resolutions

Courage and Conviction

Ethical Dilemmas, Decision-Making, and Resolutions

Lim Soo Ping

Singapore Management University, Singapore

World Scientific

NEW JERSEY · LONDON · SINGAPORE · BEIJING · SHANGHAI · HONG KONG · TAIPEI · CHENNAI · TOKYO

Published by

World Scientific Publishing Co. Pte. Ltd.

5 Toh Tuck Link, Singapore 596224

USA office: 27 Warren Street, Suite 401-402, Hackensack, NJ 07601

UK office: 57 Shelton Street, Covent Garden, London WC2H 9HE

British Library Cataloguing-in-Publication Data

A catalogue record for this book is available from the British Library.

COURAGE AND CONVICTION
Ethical Dilemmas, Decision-Making, and Resolutions

ISBN 978-981-121-189-8

For any available supplementary material, please visit
https://www.worldscientific.com/worldscibooks/10.1142/11597#t=suppl

Desk Editor: Sandhya Venkatesh

Typeset by Stallion Press
Email: enquiries@stallionpress.com

Printed in Singapore

"Through each ethical decision that we make despite the consequences, we strengthen our own character. Through each moral action that we take with courage and conviction, we make life better for others.

When we add it all up over a lifetime, we would have helped create a more resilient and caring society for our children ... and their generation."

Lim Soo Ping

ENDORSEMENTS

This short and readable book, "Courage and Conviction", is a gem. Making decisions is a part of living one's life. By its very nature, deciding is always a choice. Not deciding on a matter is a decision in itself.

In a fast pace world, deciding based on intuition is common. Often it is the end that drives the decision made. It is indeed timely for everyone to pause and reconnect with their conscience when deciding. When more decisions are given a moral weightage, we will be creating a better world.

"Courage and Conviction" provides a good framework for an individual to make better decisions. The examples given in the book help to clarify some issues in decision-making.

This is a book that I wish I had from an early age as I would not have had to work so hard on pondering such matters, and would have made better decisions in my life.

Gerard Ee
Chairman, Charities Council, Singapore
Former Nominated Member of Parliament, Singapore
Former President, Institute of Singapore
Chartered Accountants (ISCA)

Lim Soo Ping is one of our finest Auditor-Generals (AGs). The AG discharges serious financial governance oversight of our public agencies, accountable to Parliament.

In good stead, Soo Ping now passes on the value of ethical and moral considerations in decision-making. He correctly requires a high standard of care for ethical and moral financial governance. The pedagogical style and framework of this book that is tyros in content makes it readable, warm, and accessible. I commend this book to you.

Richard Magnus
Member, Public Service Commission, Singapore
Chairman, Bioethics Advisory Committee, Singapore
Vice-Chairman, UNESCO International Bioethics Committee
Retired Senior District Judge, Singapore

Lim Soo Ping has produced an insightful book on decision-making that not only documents his personal observations and views from his relevant expertise and experiences, but also invites us to self-reflect on who we are and what we stand for in the way we think, feel and behave when faced with ethical dilemmas.

By analysing the complexity in ethical situations and the bases of our responses, he shows that there is much more than what is normally labelled as courage and conviction in ethical decision-making.

Professor David Chan
Director Behavioural Sciences Institute
Singapore Management University

Ethics, as an academic subject, is often perceived as arid, ponderous, and perplexing.

Lim Soo Ping's "Courage and Conviction" debunks this myth with a thought-provoking book that is compelling, erudite, and peppered with wit. Drawn from his rich experience in the Administrative Service and academia, this book will help adjust our ethical compass.

In an ethical dilemma, Soo Ping wisely counsels "stepping back" and being mindfully aware of cognitive dissonance. His resolutely practical 6-step Dual Route Resolution Framework takes a cue from Lao Tze's aphorism: "Know thyself."

An engaging book that is meticulously researched, "Courage and Conviction" is essential reading to help us re-think the many issues that confront the ethical mind.

Professor Kua Ee Heok
Professor in Psychiatry and Neurosciences
Senior Consultant Psychiatrist
Department of Psychological Medicine
Yong Loo Lin School of Medicine
National University of Singapore

"Courage and Conviction" is a must-read book especially for professionals, such as accountants, who are confronted with ethical dilemmas in their work from time to time.

Resolving ethical dilemmas require not only conviction to remain true to one's professional code of conduct, but also the courage and fortitude to deal with the consequences of doing so.

"Courage and Conviction" provides a framework for resolving ethical dilemmas, and tips on tactical approaches as well.

This book will inspire you to make better decisions when dealing with issues with moral implications. Do read it.

Ng Boon Yew
Chartered Accountant
Executive Chairman, Raffles Campus Foundation

FOREWORD

I thank my friend, Lim Soo Ping, for asking me to contribute the foreword for his important book on ethical dilemmas, courage in decision-making, and how to serve in a big organisation, such as the civil service, without compromising one's principles or integrity.

Soo Ping was a distinguished member of the Singapore Administrative Service. He was the Auditor-General of Singapore for six years.

We face ethical dilemmas frequently, both in our work and in our life. Soo Ping has given us some examples to illustrate his approach to resolving such dilemmas. I want to share two of my recent experiences.

One day, I was having lunch with a friend at one of my social clubs. There was an altercation at the next table. A mother was having lunch with her young daughter and younger son. The son was shouting at, and kicking, his sister. The mother was unable to control him. I went over to the table and told the boy to stop kicking his sister. I told him that violence against girls and women cannot be tolerated. He quietened down and the mother took her two children outside the dining room to talk to them.

The manager of the restaurant gave me a small chocolate cake to thank me for my peace-making efforts. When the mother and her two children returned to the restaurant, I took the cake over to the boy. I asked him to apologise to his sister and to share the cake with her. He complied with my request.

What is the ethical dilemma? There is a conflict between the Singapore culture of not getting involved and my interest to make peace and to make an important point to a young man. Should I have intervened?

In another case, I was an independent director of a listed company. The management had proposed to the board to shut down our call centre and to outsource it to a foreign country. The proposal had the support of all the members of the board except me. I pointed out to the board that the employees at our call centre were our longest serving employees and we were breaking their rice bowls. I also pointed out that the amount of money saved was less than the salary of our Chief Executive Officer. I appealed to the board not to shut down our call centre. I did not succeed. Was I wrong in perceiving an ethical dilemma? Did I make the right or wrong choice? Was the board right to reject my appeal?

On courage in decision-making, I like the seven rules proposed by Soo Ping. I also like his Letter to A Young Officer. His advice to young officers is to speak up. This book is full of nuggets of wisdom.

I wish the book great success.

Tommy Koh
Professor of Law, National University of Singapore
Ambassador-At-Large, Ministry of Foreign Affairs, Singapore

ABOUT THE AUTHOR

Lim Soo Ping was Auditor-General of Singapore for six years (from 2007 to 2013). He served altogether 37 years in the Singapore Public Service. Following his retirement in early 2013, he joined the Singapore Management University (SMU) as a professor of accounting (practice) and served for six years.

In public service, Lim Soo Ping was first an engineer with the Public Works Department, serving for 13 years. He then joined the Singapore Government Administrative Service, where he served for 18 years, working in several government ministries in policy development and administration. At various times he was concurrently appointed Secretary to the Public Service Commission, Secretary to the Legal Service Commission, Secretary to the Presidential Commission of Inquiry into the collapse of Hotel New World, and Secretary to the Presidential Council for Religious Harmony.

Lim Soo Ping had his early education at St Joseph's Institution, Singapore (1957–1969). In 1974, he obtained a Bachelor of Science in Mechanical Engineering (with Distinction) from the University of Alberta (Canada) under a Colombo Plan Scholarship. In 1979 and 1981 respectively, he received a Master of Science in Industrial Engineering and a post-graduate Diploma in Business Administration, both from the University of Singapore. In 2001, he attended the Advanced Management Programme (AMP) at Harvard Business School.

In 2009, as Auditor-General, Lim Soo Ping set up the AGO[1] Academy to provide more focused training for AGO officers and serving internal auditors and finance officers in the public service as well. The Academy was officially launched by Mr S R Nathan, the then President of Singapore.

Together with fellow auditor-generals of ASEAN countries, Lim Soo Ping, is co-founder of the ASEAN Supreme Audit Institutions (ASEANSAI), a regional body of national audit institutions.[2]

Lim Soo Ping had served on the boards of directors of several government-linked organisations including Woodbridge Hospital, Tan Tock Seng Hospital, Nanyang Polytechnic, Singapore Corporation of Rehabilitative Enterprises and The Esplanade Company (Theatres on the Bay).

Outside his work in public service and SMU, Lim Soo Ping has served, for a decade, on the governing board of St Joseph's Institution International School. He was the first chairman of Equal-Ark Singapore, a charity that provides counselling support, using horse therapy, for children with learning disability and the elderly with dementia or clinical depression. Currently, he is a member of the Roman Catholic Archdiocesan Audit Committee.

---

[1] Acronym for Auditor-General's Office.

[2] ASEANSAI was officially launched on 15 November 2011 in Bali by Susilo Bambang Yudhoyono, the then President of the Republic of Indonesia and Chair of ASEAN.

PREFACE

In my six years at the Singapore Management University (SMU), I was not among the professors teaching an ethics course. It would not have crossed my mind that my first book would be on a subject focused on ethics; over the many years of my work and academic experience, my interests have been mainly in the subjects of leadership and corporate governance.

The only book on ethics that I had ever read was one that caught my attention at a book-store at Harvard Square in Boston, way back in 2001. The book "*Defining Moments*" deals with the difficult decision-making faced by managers who have to "choose between right and right". I was fascinated by the point made by the author, Professor Joseph L. Badaracco, Jr., that "… *a right-versus-right decision can reveal a manager's basic values and, in some cases, those of an organization. At the same time, the decision tests the strength of the commitments that a person or an organization has made*".[3]

I bought the book and read it over the ensuing fortnight. Thereafter, it was to remain in my bookshelf virtually untouched for almost two decades.

In late 2017, SMU Academy asked me to conduct a half-day workshop on ethical dilemmas for about 100 officers of a public institution. The Academy had assumed, rightly or wrongly, that a person who had served as auditor-general would have useful insights

---

[3] Badaracco, J. L., Jr. (1997). *Defining Moments: When Managers Must Choose between Right and Right*. Boston: Harvard Business School Press.

on the subject. I conducted the workshop commencing with a plenary session where I gave a talk on ethical dilemmas using case studies based mostly on personal observations and experience.

In preparing for the workshop, I reviewed various literature on ethics and ethical dilemmas. These helped me understand better moral reasoning and the nature of ethical dilemmas. It gave me some confidence in conducting the workshop.

Unexpectedly, over the next four months after the workshop, I received three invitations to speak on the subject, two from government ministries and one from a professional body on internal auditing. Encouraged by this, and following suggestions from a few friends, I decided that I should document, in a book, my thoughts on this fascinating subject. During the university mid-year break in 2018, I started writing, gathering my thoughts along the way, especially on plane and train rides during my vacation.

There are many excellent publications and commentaries on the handling of ethical dilemmas. I have learned much from them. In this book, I am primarily sharing my own perspectives based on personal observations. My approach is quite similar to how I teach at SMU, namely explaining concepts and illustrating them with anecdotes and cases.

This book opens with a discussion on the nature of ethical dilemmas and moral reasoning. Different aspects of an ethical dilemma and its handling are examined in separate chapters to enable deeper understanding. A guide for resolving ethical dilemmas is presented in two chapters. Ensuing chapters look at ethical dilemmas in the context of professional work, running corporations, and public service. The book ends with a discussion on a common ethical dilemma, namely, answering an "inconvenient question", and on morality in decision-making for a person exercising authority.

Provided at the end of each chapter is a summary of the key learning points and one or more questions for readers to reflect on, to deepen their understanding of the concepts and their application.

I hope that readers will find this book of some use in their personal and professional life, and that they would also share any insights from it with their friends and colleagues. I welcome all feedback from readers.

Happy reading.

Lim Soo Ping

ACKNOWLEDGEMENTS

This book would not have been possible without the support and assistance of many friends and colleagues.

First and foremost, I am very grateful for the warm and inspiring foreword written by Professor Tommy Koh.

I thank Professor David Chan for his insightful comments on the content, clarity, and coherence of arguments in the book, and suggestions on how to frame concepts adequately.

I am grateful to Dr Lim Lai Cheng, Director of SMU Academy and my former public service colleague, for "volunteering" me to conduct a workshop on ethical dilemmas, thereby sparking my profound interest in the subject, leading to the writing this book.

I thank Mr Gerard Ee, Mr Richard Magnus, Professor Kua Ee Heok and Mr Ng Boon Yew for their encouragement and kind words in endorsing the book.

I acknowledge with thanks the comments and suggestions from Professor Leong Kwong Sin and Associate Professor Gary Pan on the structure and flow of the substance of the book.

My gratitude goes to Linette Heng for her meticulous assistance with editing; Karen Cheah, Della Ng and Michael K H Chan for their suggestions to make the book more interesting and useful; and Michael Lim Guanzhong, my youngest son, for his artwork within the pages of the book.

My special thanks go to my former SMU students, Lee Wanyun, Bryan Er, Sheriel Chia Yun Zhen and Gladys Lim Jiewei. They spent many hours reading the manuscript at various stages, and provided me with comments and suggestions from the perspective of young professionals, contributed anecdotes, and helped with the editing work.

I thank SMU School of Accountancy for the administrative resources for my teaching and writing. I thank SMU Library for helping me with comments and assistance regarding citations in the book.

Above all, I acknowledge, with deep gratitude, the support that I received for many years from the late Mr S R Nathan, the former President of Singapore. Mr Nathan inspired me to spend my post-retirement years nurturing our next generation through teaching at SMU.

CONTENTS

1. INTRODUCTION

Elsie[1], a friend who runs a training institution for executives, once asked for my advice on an "ethical dilemma" that she was facing. Her institution recently introduced a new course and engaged Matthew, an independent trainer, to teach the course and also help promote it through his own network. Matthew would receive a fee for each course participant he introduced.

Matthew subsequently submitted to Elsie a list of names of persons to whom he claimed he had introduced the course. The list would be his basis for his claim of introduction fees. The names in the list would be matched to those of applicants for the course.

Elsie found that three persons on Matthew's list, in their course application forms, named another person, Raj, as introducer. When she enquired, Matthew explained that Raj had been a participant of several of his own courses, and he therefore, felt entitled to the introduction fees. Moreover, Raj, a bank executive, was not claiming any introduction fees.

Intuitively, Elsie felt that it was not proper to pay Matthew the introduction fees for the three cases. However, she was also loath to losing the goodwill of Matthew who might perceive her as quibbling over a trivial matter.

I suggested to Elsie that she should require Matthew to declare in his fee claim that Raj was acting as his "agent", explaining that this was necessary for "audit purpose". She followed my advice. Unsurprisingly,

---

[1] No names are used in this case.

1

Matthew decided not to pursue the matter. Elsie's "ethical dilemma" was thus, resolved.

We all face ethical dilemmas in our personal and work life from time to time. Elsie's dilemma was a relatively straightforward one, and a simple tactical approach had helped resolve it with no consequences. The resolution helped Elsie to avoid having to decide between breaching a financial rule (making an improper payment) and the loss of goodwill of a partner of the institution.

However, an ethical dilemma that one might face can also be immensely troubling. One might lose sleep over it as there might be no easy way out of it, or no way to avoid the consequences of one's decision.

Ethical Dilemma *vis-a-vis* Moral Dilemma

The terms "ethical dilemma" and "moral dilemma" are often used interchangeably, but there is an important difference between them. The word "ethics" relates to rules laid down by society or a community to govern the conduct of its members, such as state laws, company policies, and the codes of ethical conduct for doctors, accountants, and other professionals. The word "morality" is somewhat different. It relates to a person's value system that helps him discern between right and wrong.

An "ethical dilemma" is a conundrum between the breaking of a rule and the pursuit of a moral principle, whereas a "moral dilemma" involves a conflict between two moral principles.

This book deals principally with "ethical dilemmas". In an ethical dilemma (as also in a moral dilemma), neither of the two decision paths is unambiguously more acceptable than the other. There are consequences, whichever way one decides. Two persons facing the same predicament might make different decisions. The deciding factor is the person himself, in particular, his values and belief system and his strength of character.

An ethical dilemma can be described as making a decision between "Right" and "Right".

Ethical dilemmas make for excellent themes in stories and movies. Consider the movie *"The Light Between Oceans"*[2] where, in the story, a young couple manning a lighthouse found an infant and a dead man in a dinghy that washed ashore. The wife had just had a miscarriage. The couple, assuming that the dead man was the infant's father and that the mother had drowned, decided to take the child as their own. A few years later, the husband spotted a woman grieving at a grave. When he later read the headstone, he realised that the woman was grieving over the loss of her husband and baby at sea, on the same day that the couple found the baby. The man found himself in an ethical dilemma — he has to decide whether to return the child to its biological mother thus, breaking the heart of his wife, or run afoul of the law by not reporting the finding of the infant.

In another movie, *"Eye In The Sky"*,[3] in an anti-terrorist operation, an aerial bombing of a terrorist hideout in a village was about to commence when a young girl suddenly appeared and set up a stall just outside the hideout to sell bread that her mother had baked. The commander of the operation had to decide whether to execute the mission as ordered or to delay it at some risk of mission failure.

The posters for both movies show the main characters with troubled expressions, reflecting the state of mind of anyone caught in an ethical dilemma.

Consider a hypothetical case of an ethical dilemma in a workplace situation. Jason is the CEO of a building construction

---

[2] Cianfrance, D. (2016). The Light Between Oceans. Walt Disney Studios Motion Pictures. *The Light Between Oceans* is a 2016 film based on a novel by M. L. Stedman published by Random House of Australia in 2012.
[3] Hood, G. (2015). Eye In The Sky. Entertainment One. *Eye In The Sky is* a 2015 film starring Helen Mirren, *et al*, based on a story by Guy Hibbert.

company. He received a memo from his foreman informing him that two employees, electricians Kim Jae and Jack Soh, were caught taking drugs at a worksite. The foreman asked Jason for his decision on whether to file a report to the anti-narcotics agency.

Jason is aware that the two employees, both in their late 20s, have been good performers in their jobs. He also knows that Kim is the only child and breadwinner in his family. But, under the company's policy, suspected unlawful activities are to be referred to the relevant law enforcement authority.

The company has no precedent cases of this nature to serve as reference for Jason's decision-making. The foreman, when he brought the matter to Jason's attention, suggested that the two employees just be given a warning.

Jason is thus, caught in an ethical dilemma. He knows that, rightly, he should report the matter to the authorities pursuant to company's policy. On the other hand, the drug taking, while criminal, had caused no loss to the company. In fact, Kim and Jack have had no work performance issues. In the case of Kim, should he be prosecuted for drug consumption, this would affect his family as he is the sole breadwinner. It might also be argued that drug consumption is a victimless offence, the harm done being only to the offender himself.

In this case, in conflict are the principle of compliance with company policy and the moral value of compassion. Whichever way Jason decides, there are consequences. If he files a report with the authorities, a family will suffer hardship. On the other hand, if Jason refrains from doing so, he would be setting a bad example of not complying with a company policy.

Dealing with an Ethical Dilemma

An ethical dilemma is a complex situation. When facing one, a person should not simply adhere to a policy or rule as a matter of absolute duty or obligation, nor should one simply flout it out of bravado in the name of morality. Resolving an ethical dilemma is a process of navigating the complexity of issues, options, and consequences to choose the path that leads to a more acceptable, or the less unacceptable, outcome, having regard for one's moral values and strength of character to deal or live with the consequences.

The next chapter looks at concepts of moral reasoning that provide an insight into the psychological factors that influence decision-making in an ethical dilemma.

Summary

- All of us face ethical or moral dilemmas from time to time in our personal life or work life.

- An "ethical dilemma" involves making a choice between complying with a law, rule, or policy and upholding a moral principle.

- A "moral dilemma" is different. It involves making a choice between two moral principles.

- Resolving an ethical dilemma is a process of navigating issues and considering options, having regard for one's moral values and strength of character to deal or live with the consequences.

Question for Reflection

Recall an ethical or moral dilemma that you have faced or observed. What were the circumstances that made it troubling for the decision maker? How was it resolved?

NATURE OF AN ETHICAL DILEMMA

2. ETHICAL DILEMMAS

An ethical dilemma is a situation where a choice has to be made between two courses of action neither of which, from a moral and ethical perspective, is unambiguously more acceptable than the other. To get a deeper insight into the nature of ethical dilemmas, let us consider three scenarios.

Scenario 1

James is testifying in a court of law in a case where the accused is a close friend. If James were to tell the whole truth, it would jeopardise his friend's case. On the other hand, to be untruthful is to commit perjury, an offence punishable by law. James is caught between complying with the law and upholding loyalty to a close friend.

Scenario 2[1]

In 1884, two British sailors, Tom Dudley and Edwin Stephens, were shipwrecked in a lifeboat along with one other sailor and a 17-year old cabin boy, an orphan.

By their third week adrift, the little amount of food and water that they salvaged from their ship had run out. The cabin boy had fallen into a coma and was dying. Dudley and Stephens contemplated killing him to consume his blood for survival. The other sailor did not want to be involved.

---

[1] R V Dudley and Stephens (1884) 14 QBD 273 DC.

9

Dudley and Stephens were in an extreme ethical dilemma, having to decide between killing a person and their own eventual death through thirst and starvation. In the end, after considering that imminent rescue was unlikely, that the cabin boy was on the verge of death, and that he was an orphan, the two decided to proceed with the deed.

Days later, unexpectedly, a ship passed by and the sailors were rescued. When they were brought back to England, all three were candid in their statements to the authorities, as required under the Merchant Shipping Act in the event of a shipping loss. They had believed that they were protected by a custom of the sea that provided for an act of life sacrifice through the drawing of lots in an extreme survival situation. Instead, they were both arrested and put on trial for murder. Rejecting their defence of "necessity", the trial court found Dudley and Stephens guilty of murder. The two were sentenced to death. However, considering the circumstances of the case, the court also recommended clemency. The sentences were commuted to six months imprisonment for each of them.

Scenario 3

This hypothetical case is from an article in The Straits Times, titled "Lessons on the Use of Torture",[2] by Professor Simon Chesterman. The article presented this scenario: *"Imagine a scenario in which a terrorist has planted a bomb that will detonate within a fixed period of time and kill a large number of people. The terrorist has been apprehended but will not reveal the location of the bomb. Should any restrictions limit the interrogation? Can the terrorist be tortured?"* The consequence of not applying

---

[2] Simon Chesterman, *Lessons on the Use of Torture* (The Straits Times, December 17, 2014). Professor Simon Chesterman is Dean and Professor of Law at the National University of Singapore.

torture is the probable loss of many innocent lives. On the other hand, if torture is used, the interrogators would face prosecution and a jail sentence.

Two main factors make ethical dilemmas troubling. Firstly, how one decides depends on one's value system and strength of character. There is no decision science method to point the decision maker to the right direction. Secondly, there are consequences for the decision maker whichever way he decides.

The scenarios above indicate that an action that is moral is not necessarily legal. Conversely, an act that is legal is not necessarily moral. This is the genesis of an ethical dilemma.

A Generic Definition of Ethical Dilemma

For the purpose of this book, I broadly define an ethical dilemma as a "Conflict between a Code of Morality and a Code of Conduct".

"Code of Morality" encompasses such concepts as one's own moral values and conscience (the "inner voice"). Morality is personal and normative, and it speaks of one's sense of right and wrong, and what ought to be. These qualities may stem from one's religion, family upbringing, culture and tradition, education, and life experiences. The manifestations of morality would be such values as mercy, compassion, justice, fairness, loyalty, goodwill, and harmony.

"Code of Conduct" refers to standards of right and wrong established by a society or organisation that their members are required to uphold and comply with. Some examples are state laws, company policies, codes of conduct of professions, and customs and traditions. Code of Conduct also encompasses the "right" of a person, e.g. legal right and contractual right.

Consequences

Consequences are a defining feature of an ethical dilemma. It is what makes an ethical dilemma troubling for the decision maker.

The consequences of breaching a Code of Conduct include prosecution, legal sanction, disciplinary action, censure of sorts, and financial hardship. The consequences of breaching a Code of Morality include human suffering, loss of friendship or goodwill, loss of trust and respect, and shame.

Rosie was walking along a sidewalk outside the National Art Gallery when she caught sight of a $20 note stuck in the grating of a pavement gutter. There was no one else around and she picked up the note and walked away. Rosie was momentarily in an ethical dilemma. She knew that she had no right to the money. Should she turn it in at the nearest police station or to the Lost & Found department of the National Art Gallery, or keep it for herself as she could do with some extra cash? It was not a large amount of money after all, and the owner might not even be missing it.

This ethical dilemma is not a very troubling one for Rosie as the consequences, if any, were not serious as no one was watching. Of course, Rosie also has the option to donate the money to charity and this would have satisfied her conscience.

But in other ethical dilemmas, the consequences can be dire. In the hypothetical case of the use of torture to obtain information from a captured terrorist (from Scenario 3), the consequences would be criminal prosecution if torture is applied, or the loss of many innocent lives if torture is not applied.

Consequences can affect other persons, not just the decision maker. For example, in the earlier case in Chapter 1, of Jason, the CEO of the construction company who has to decide whether to report the two employees suspected to have consumed narcotics drugs, the other parties who would be affected were the families of the employees, one of whom was a sole breadwinner.

Mitigation of Consequences

It might be possible to mitigate the effects of consequences to reduce or soften their negative impact, thereby making decision-making easier.

In 2005, Singapore as a society experienced a great ethical dilemma at national level. In an unprecedented move, the Government announced its intention to allow casino gambling to boost the economy and help make it more sustainable.

Parliament debated the issue for months. The proposal to allow two "integrated resorts" with casinos was opposed by some religious and social groups that feared the consequences of social ills, including gambling addiction and crime. This would affect individual citizens, families and the clean and wholesome image of Singapore as a country.

It was an ethical dilemma of epic proportion between an economic imperative on one hand, and the preservation of the social and moral well-being of the population on the other. Parliament was divided on the issue.

To minimise the negative social impact of casino gambling, the Government proposed "comprehensive measures" as safeguards to mitigate the social ills of gambling. These included requiring a hefty entrance levy for locals, and having casino exclusions and visit limits to prevent problem gamblers and persons in financial hardship from entering, or frequenting, a casino in Singapore. With such mitigating measures in place, the proposal to allow casinos was eventually approved by Parliament.

In trying to resolve an ethical dilemma, one should always try to mitigate the consequences of each decision path.

Summary

- A moral act is not necessarily a legal act. Conversely, a legal act is not necessarily a moral act. It is the conflict between legality and morality in a situation that gives rise to an ethical dilemma.

- An ethical dilemma may be seen as a conflict between a Code of Morality and a Code of Conduct.

- The manifestations of a Code of Morality include mercy, compassion, justice, fairness, loyalty, goodwill, and harmony.

- The manifestations of a Code of Conduct include state laws, company policies, the codes of conduct of professions, and customs and traditions.

- Consequences are what make an ethical dilemma troubling for the decision maker.

- The typical consequences of breaching a Code of Conduct include legal sanction, disciplinary proceeding, some form of censure, and financial hardship.

- The typical consequences of breaching a Code of Morality include human suffering, loss of friendship or goodwill, unfairness, loss of trust and respect, loss of reputation, and shame.

- In resolving an ethical dilemma, one should always try to mitigate the consequences of each decision path. This may help make the decision-making easier.

Questions for Reflection

1. *Recall an ethical dilemma that you have encountered in your personal life or work life. What were the decision choices and the consequences of each choice? What was your decision in the end? Do you feel, on hindsight, that you made the right choice, or you could have done better?*

2. *Imagine that you are a CEO who is making a decision that would result in a staff member not getting the promotion that he has been expecting. You know that he would be extremely disappointed and his work morale would be affected. What can you do to soften the impact on him?*

3. MORAL REASONING

A human being is a moral creature because of his innate ability to make value judgments and to choose between alternative courses of action. He does so with the awareness of the consequences of each action, and having regard for the socio-economic environment that he is in.

In an ethical dilemma, one might make a decision instinctively. However, when the consequences are grave, the ethical dilemma becomes daunting and has to be more carefully resolved. How does one consciously make a moral judgement and act on it? What guides one's moral reasoning process?

The Trolley Thought Experiment

In 1967, British philosopher Philippa Foot[1] developed a thought experiment for the teaching of moral reasoning. The thought experiment was extensively analysed by other researchers and variants of it has been popularly used. The general scenario is as follows: You are the driver of a runaway trolley and you see five people on the track ahead. You can either steer the trolley onto a side track where there is one person on it or allow it to continue on its present track. How would you decide?

A decision to switch track reflects the Utilitarian Principle[2] of moral reasoning. The principle says that an act is moral if it results

---

[1] Philippa Ruth Foot (1920–2010) was a British philosopher.
[2] The first systematic account of Utilitarianism was developed by Jeremy Bentham (1748–1832).

in the greatest benefit for the greatest number of people. Utilitarianism is a branch of the Consequentialism[3] theory of moral reasoning that propounds that the morality of an act is judged by its outcome. In other words, the end justifies the means.

The trolley driver, seeing that there is also a person on the other track, might decide to do nothing and allow the trolley to continue on its present track. Such a decision comes under the Deontological Principle[4] of moral reasoning. This principle says that the morality of an action should be based on whether that action in itself is right or wrong, regardless of its consequences. Hence, under the Deontological Principle of moral reasoning, to switch track would be morally wrong as it is tantamount to a deliberate action to kill a person.

In my talks on ethical dilemmas, I presented the trolley thought experiment prior to talking about the principles of moral reasoning, to see how the participants would decide if they were the trolley driver. The poll result averaged over three talks is as follows:

> I will switch track: 53%
> I will not switch track: 47%

The poll result reflects the defining characteristic of an ethical dilemma: There is no unambiguously correct answer. It can be said that both decisions are equally right (or equally wrong).

Generally speaking, the Deontological Principle relates to persons whose actions are bound by some form of code of ethical conduct, such as doctors, lawyers, and accountants. For other situations, both the Deontological Principle and Consequentialism Principle would apply, depending on the value system of the decision maker.

---

[3] The term "Consequentialism" was introduced by British philosopher Elizabeth Anscombe in 1958.
[4] Immanuel Kant (1724–1804), a German philosopher, was the first to define the Deontological Principle of moral reasoning.

Take the earlier scenario of Jason, the CEO of the construction firm, who has to decide whether to comply with the company's policy and report the two drug-taking young employees to the authorities with consequences on their families. Jason's decision would turn on what he would consider to be a more desirable outcome. He might take the Deontological approach if he deems compliance with a company policy to be sacrosanct. If instead he decides not to report the two employees out of compassion, he would be taking the Consequentialism approach. In different ways, both decisions are principled decisions.

In the next chapter, we shall examine what might help trip the balance between the two decision paths in an ethical dilemma.

Summary

- There are two main principles in moral reasoning: the Consequentialism Principle and Deontological Principle.

- Under the Consequentialism Principle, an act is moral if its outcome is desirable and benefits the greatest number of people.

- Under the Deontological Principle, an act is moral if it is intrinsically moral, even if its outcome is not desirable.

- Generally, the Deontological Principle applies to persons whose actions are subjected to a code of ethical conduct that he has pledged to uphold. Such persons include doctors, lawyers, accountants, auditors, and engineers.

- In a general situation, the decision taken can reflect either one of the two principles of moral reasoning. This depends on the character and value system of the decision maker.

Question for Reflection

You intend to donate a violin to a deserving student of a school. The school presents two students for your choosing. One student is a good violin player who has been training very hard; he is using an old violin of modest quality. The other student is an aspiring violin player from a poor family; he is using a borrowed violin.

How would you decide who should get your violin?

RESOLVING AN
ETHICAL DILEMMA

4. COURAGE AND CONVICTION

"Plainly, it does not suffice for integrity that we come to our own views about the principles and values we wish to endorse and act upon. Beyond that, it is essential that we have the courage to stand up for those views and defend them against external pressures and influences even when the consequences of doing so might be professionally and personally risky."[1]

— Sundaresh Menon
Chief Justice of Singapore

In an ethical dilemma, which decision path one chooses would depend on where one's greater conviction lie and whether one is prepared to face the attendant consequences of the decision being taken.

A person's conviction on a matter reflects his value system that is founded on his upbringing and shaped by his life experiences. His sense of right and wrong would guide his decision-making. Having a strong sense of morality would steer him towards upholding a moral principle. Otherwise, one's natural instinct would be to take the path with fewer consequences.

A former student of mine, Sharon[2] shared her story. A year into her new job, she faced an ethical dilemma. She was asked by her supervisor to inflate the quarterly performance results of the department in order to be seen as meeting its quarterly target.

---

[1] Menon, S. (2015). The Integrity of Judges. In the 15th Biennial Conference of Chief Justices of Asia and the Pacific. Core Values of an Effective Judiciary. Singapore: Academy Publishing, Chapter 1, p. 12.
[2] Not her real name.

Sharon was not willing to cooperate for ethical reasons. Eventually, the supervisor himself made the false reporting. However, Sharon decided to leave the firm as she could not accept such lack of integrity in the management. She shared with me that she could bear the consequences of her decision (loss of job and income), but she also wondered whether she would have decided differently if she were the sole breadwinner in the family.

I told Sharon that she had acted with conviction when the circumstances made it untenable for her to continue in her position.

Conviction Softeners

In an ethical dilemma, one's conviction can be weakened by what I would call "conviction softeners". Sharon's supervisor, sensing her reluctance to co-operate, explained that the inflation was an advanced recognition of performance expected in the next reporting period. The supervisor assured Sharon that he would take full responsibility since she would be acting under his instruction. Sharon did not accept his assurance, recognising that it was intended to soften her conviction to uphold her professional integrity.

In the final lecture of my auditing course at the Singapore Management University, I touch on ethical dilemmas using a case study based on the story in the 1991 Hollywood movie, *Scent of a Woman*[3]. In the plot, the car of the principal of a college was vandalised by a group of students. The principal wanted a student, Charlie Sims, who happened to be in the vicinity the previous night when the culprits were setting up the prank, to divulge the identities of the perpetrators. When Charlie refused, the principal tried to weaken Charlie's conviction of loyalty to his friends, by offering a recommendation for a scholarship to a prestigious university.

---

[3] Brest, M. (1992). *Scent of a Woman*. Universal Pictures. *Scent of a Woman* is an American drama film produced by Martin Brest, starring Al Pacino, based on the novel *Il buio e il miele* by Giovanni Arpino.

Charlie could have accepted the bribe as his family was too poor to pay for his university education. However, he stood firm in his conviction that it would be wrong to betray friends for a bribe.

Charlie later found himself in a worse ethical dilemma that put his conviction to a greater test.

Courage

Conviction in itself might not be sufficient, especially when the consequences are dire. While conviction points one to the right door, it is courage that causes one to open that door and to walk through it.

In the very memorable final scene of *Scent of a Woman*, Charlie was being questioned on the matter again, this time in an open inquiry. When he maintained his stance not to disclose whom he saw setting up the prank, the principal threatened him with expulsion. Notwithstanding the dire consequences, Charlie continued to stand his ground. The character Frank Slade, a blind retired army colonel, who was at the inquiry then spoke up for Charlie in a strong and forthright manner. He said that while he did not know whether Charlie's silence was right or wrong, he noted that Charlie would not betray his friends to "buy his future". He said *"That, my friend, is called 'integrity'. That's called 'courage'."*

Courage in Real Life

A real life story about courage in an ethical dilemma in the corporate world impresses me. This concerns WorldCom, a very large telecommunications corporation that was mired in a major accounting scandal in 2002.

Cynthia Cooper was the Vice President of Internal Audit at WorldCom at that time. She faced administrative obstacles and veiled threats from certain key management personnel because of the thorough and astute manner in which she did her job of auditing the financial transactions and records of the company. There was even a threat to reduce the headcount of her internal audit department. She endured the monumentally challenging work environment. With perseverance and determination, she and her team uncovered a major accounting fraud in the company. When the fraud became public, following investigations by the authorities, the company's stock price plummeted. WorldCom filed for bankruptcy protection in 2002, and tens of thousands of employees lost their jobs. The former CEO and various other senior executives of the company were convicted of securities fraud and sentenced to imprisonment.

In her book, *Extraordinary Circumstances: The Journey of a Corporate Whistleblower*, Cynthia Cooper recounted "*how easy it is to rationalize, give in to fear, and cave under pressure and intimidation*".[4] She also spoke of the value of having strong integrity and moral boundaries as well as the importance of making decisions one can look back on without regret. She says in the preface of her book: "*I found myself standing at a crossroads. Looking back, I would take the same path again. But doing the right thing doesn't mean there will be no cost to others, your family, or yourself.*"[5]

Sources of Courage

Courage is the character trait of a person that drives him to act according to his conviction in the face of opposition, disapproval, or other consequences. What is the source of courage? Is courage, or the lack of it, inherent in a person? I do not think so. I see three determinants of courage, namely: Conviction, Fortitude and Moral Support.

"Conviction" is a fundamental prerequisite for courage. Without conviction, there is no courage (but maybe just foolhardiness).

[4] Cooper, C. (2008). *Extraordinary Circumstances: The Journey of a Whistleblower.* New Jersey: Wiley, p. 362.
[5] Cooper, C. (2008). *Extraordinary Circumstances: The Journey of a Whistleblower.* New Jersey: Wiley, p. ix.

"Fortitude" is a character trait that enables a person to bear, or even live with, the consequences of acting on his conviction. Not everyone with strong conviction on a matter would have the fortitude to bear the consequences of acting on that conviction. For example, an executive may not be prepared to resign to uphold his principle of integrity if he were the sole breadwinner in the family. He would have to secure a new job first.

"Moral Support" refers to the emotional support that comes from family and friends. This is especially important when one makes a decision that is controversial and has dire consequences on the decision maker. It does not necessarily mean that the family and friends must agree with the decision made, but they are there to provide comfort and moral support.

Rationalisation

If the decision maker lacks the courage or conviction to uphold a moral principle, he might use different ways to justify to himself, or to others, why he is taking that path. Consider the following example.

Kate, a purchasing officer of a company, was asked by her supervisor to accept as valid a bid that was received one day past the deadline. The supervisor told her that the supplier had explained to him that they missed the deadline because of severe staff shortage in their sales unit and it was the first time they were late in submitting a bid.

Kate knew that it was improper to accept a bid that came after the submission deadline. To do so would be unfair to the other bidders. However, she eventually agreed to do as asked by the supervisor. She reasoned that the deadline was missed by just one day, and that all the bids received on time have not yet been opened for evaluation. She also took comfort in the fact that it was in effect her supervisor who made the decision to accept the late bid.

What Kate did was wrong and she knew that. It was to justify her conscience that she came up with those reasons for her action. This is rationalisation. The reasons were "constructed" to justify her decision to go along with her supervisor when she could have said no.

Rationalisation

Rationalisation occurs in two steps. First, a decision is taken for a reason, for example, out of fear of a consequence or for convenience. Then, a justification is constructed based on seemingly rational or logical grounds.

Acts of rationalisation are not uncommon in life, but usually not recognised as such until it is pointed out. Here are some examples of statements based on rationalisation:

- *"There is no need to look further into the matter as the employee who complained is leaving the company."*
- *"There is no need to review the disciplinary decision with the new evidence since the accused is not appealing."*
- *"We should accept the situation as it could have been far worse."*
- *"Disclosing the full facts in the statement might undermine public confidence in the company."*

A rationalisation is an explanation that seems or sounds plausible. However, it might actually be at odds with logic if one studies it closely. Consider this example: A municipality has decided that public parking charges in the city are to be raised because of the rising cost of construction and maintenance. As this would be an unpopular decision, an extra reason is added in the public communication, namely, that it is necessary to bring the city's public parking charges in line with those of other cities in the country. One can question the logic of this argument: Are cars coming from other cities to take undue advantage of the lower parking charges in this city?

In my auditing course, I teach my students to distinguish between "reason" and "rationalisation" when an explanation for a financial lapse is given to the auditor by the management of the company being audited. Auditors know that explanations for lapses should not be accepted at face value, but viewed with a dose of professional scepticism.

The next chapter looks at resolving ethical dilemmas, taking into account the role of courage and conviction.

Summary

- In an ethical dilemma, one might have the conviction to take the moral path.

- Courage and fortitude are necessary for the decision maker to act on that conviction.

- The essential ingredients for courage are Conviction, Fortitude, and Moral Support (of family and friends).

- If a decision is based not on Conviction, but on Convenience, the decision maker might resort to rationalisation to explain his decision.

- Rationalisation serves only to make the decision maker feel better for a decision already taken.

- A telltale sign of rationalisation is that the explanation might be at odds with logic.

Question for Reflection

John, the head of the finance section, is trying to summon up enough courage to tell his boss, the director of finance, that it is improper that he made an unsupported adjustment to an accounting record. John did not want to use the company's whistleblower channel as the monetary value of the adjustment was small (only about $3,000).

John seeks your advice on how he should talk to his director? What is your advice?

5. RESOLUTION: GENERAL FRAMEWORK

Framing an Ethical Dilemma

At a young age, I heard an interesting anecdote about a monk in a monastery. The monk was a compulsive smoker and he found the daily prayer sessions to be particularly trying without his pipe. One day, he asked the Abbot: "May one smoke when praying?" The Abbot answered with an emphatic "No". Months later, the monk decided to ask the Abbot again, but this time in a different way: "May one pray while smoking?" The Abbot replied: "Yes, of course."

How one frames a question affects how it is answered. This applies also to resolving an ethical dilemma. Being able to identify, and present upfront, the basic principles in conflict, instead of the actions in conflict, provides clarity on what is at stake. This enables more effective decision-making. Consider the following hypothetical scenario.

Jean is the operations manager of Fun-at-Farm (FAF), a special school that provides experiential learning for children in an animal farm setting. FAF occupies a small plot of land rented from a large commercial farm. The facilities of FAF were undergoing a major renovation. The day after the renovation started, a farmhand found that a passage in the FAF premises, that he has been using as a short cut, was obstructed by construction materials. In anger the farmhand, who was known to be a loutish person, brandished an axe, shouted at the staff of FAF, and threatened to set fire to the construction materials if they were not removed.

Jean immediately brought the matter to the attention of her executive director. An urgent meeting was held and it went this way:

Jean: "We have two options. The first is to report the matter to the police. The second is to report it to the landlord. If we make a police report, our landlord, being an unreasonable person, would likely be upset. We should show him some deference. However, if we just report the incident to him and not the police, I am not sure that he would take it seriously and rebuke and control the farmhand."

Executive Director: "Is there a downside to just reporting the matter to the landlord? Isn't the threat by the farmhand serious enough to warrant making a police report?"

Jean: "Well, if we report the matter to the landlord and he does not act on it, we can't later make a police report. That would really upset him. Another downside is that our staff would not feel safe. The farmhand made a threat. I don't see why we should acquiesce and move the construction material just because he needs a short cut."

Kay (another manager): "I think the safety and morale of our staff are very important. We are responsible for their welfare. Our landlord might be unhappy if we report the matter to the police, but we can explain to him our concern about the safety of our staff."

Executive Director: "From what I hear, it seems to me that our decision choices are not between making a police report and complaining to the landlord, but between showing deference to the landlord and upholding staff morale and safety. This is what is really at stake. It seems clear to me that staff morale takes precedent."

With the ethical dilemma reframed, the meeting was able to make its decision with greater clarity and conviction. A police report was made, but at the same time, the landlord was kept informed to mitigate any misunderstanding or negative feelings he might have. The matter was decisively resolved.

Resolving Ethical Dilemmas

Resolving an ethical dilemma hinges primarily on human values and human factors. The resolution methods for ethical dilemmas that I have come across typically require the identification of the applicable laws and other obligations, the parties affected, the consequences of each course of action, and how a decision would come across to affected parties or the public, e.g. on social media. A list of questions on these aspects is presented for the decision maker to ponder over, after which he would make his decision.

I propose a resolution process where a key step is to frame the ethical dilemma in terms of a conflict between a code of morality and a code of conduct.

Code of Morality & Code of Conduct (from Chapter 2)

"Code of Morality" encompasses such concepts as one's own moral values and conscience (the "inner voice"). Morality is personal and normative, and it speaks of one's sense of right and wrong, and what ought to be. These qualities stem from one's religion, family upbringing, culture and tradition, education, or life experiences. The manifestations of morality would be such values as mercy, compassion, justice, fairness, loyalty, goodwill, and harmony.

"Code of Conduct" refers to standards of right and wrong established by a society or organisation, that their members are required to uphold and comply with. Some examples are state laws, company policies, codes of conduct of professions, and customs and traditions. A Code of Conduct also encompasses the "right" of a person, e.g. legal right and contractual right.

To the representative list of Codes of Conduct, I would add "Protocol" and "Right of Discretion".

"Protocol" refers to an unwritten rule that has come about in an organisation for some reason, for example, an undocumented requirement by the CEO of a company that a certain category of spending decisions must have his concurrence, even though, under written rules, the managers have full authority of their own to make such decisions.

A protocol might be only a perceived one. It could have arisen from a verbal comment made by a dominant CEO in the course of discussing a case. The functionaries then took that to be a rule to be followed for all similar cases, even if the CEO had not intended this. The irony is that, being undocumented, a protocol is not subjected to review and can therefore, be more enduring than documented rules. It takes an astute (and courageous) executive to question the validity of such a protocol.

"Right of Discretion" refers to one's right not to act in a situation called a Bystander Dilemma, e.g. to offer assistance to a person in need, when there is ability, but no legal obligation, to do so. (Bystander Dilemma is dealt with in Chapter 6.)

Dual Route Resolution Framework

The resolution method proposed, the "Dual Route Resolution Framework" is based on the premise that the decision maker desires to uphold the Code of Morality act in the first instance. Whether he actually chooses that path depends on how able and prepared he is to face the attendant consequences. It requires conviction, and the courage to act on the conviction, in the face of the consequences.

The steps in the Dual Route Resolution Framework are as follows:

STEP 1: Gathering information

Obtain all relevant information, namely (a) the background information, (b) the applicable law, policy, rule, etc., (c) the moral principles that might be compromised, e.g. mercy, compassion, fairness, loyalty, goodwill, etc., and (d) the parties potentially affected by the decision to be made.

STEP 2: Framing the ethical dilemma

Frame the ethical dilemma in the form of Code of Conduct versus Code of Morality (instead of Action A versus Action B). This brings out starkly the principles that are in conflict, thereby providing greater clarity and focus in the decision-making.

STEP 3: Identifying the consequences

Identify the consequences that come with each decision path. A consequence might be legal, economic, physical or social (or a combination of these) in nature, e.g. legal or disciplinary sanction, censure, economic or financial hardship, danger to life, embarrassment, damage to reputation, loss of goodwill, etc. Identify and consider measures for mitigating the consequences.

STEP 4: Asking yourself: "Who am I?"

In an ethical dilemma, the decision taken reveals the character of the decision maker. Ask yourself these questions:

- *"What do I stand for?"*
- *"Do I have the conviction to pursue the path of morality?"*
- *"Do I have the courage to act on that conviction despite the consequences?"*

The General

I remember the memorable lines in a scene from a war movie that I watched on television in the 1970s. I cannot recall the title of the movie and the actors.

(Continued)

(Continued)

> It was an early morning during the last months of World War II. A US army general was getting ready to launch an invasion of a heavily fortified Pacific island. In a moment of introspection, as he was donning his uniform, he asked his aide-de-camp (ADC): "Today, thousands will lose their lives in this operation that I planned. What does that make me?"
>
> The ADC replied: "That makes you a general, Sir."

STEP 5: Choosing your decision path

After having considered the decision paths and the consequences, and taking into account your own value system, make your decision.

STEP 6: Confirming your decision

Before executing the decision, it is useful to do a final check. A good test is the "sleep test". Can one sleep well with the decision made?

I would add two other tests, namely, the public inquiry test and the eulogy test. At a public inquiry (e.g. into an incident affecting public safety), the questioning of the responsible parties involved by the inquiry panel is to establish whether they had acted in accordance with their duties, and conducted themselves with integrity and in the public interest. Ask oneself: "Can the decision that I made in this ethical dilemma stand up to such public scrutiny?"

In the eulogy test, the question is whether the way one handled the ethical dilemma is worthy of mention in one's eulogy, or too shameful to be mentioned.

Dilemmas Resolution for Professionals

Where the decision maker is a person under a specific obligation to act in the public interest, namely, professionals such as lawyers,

doctors, accountants, auditors, and engineers, there is a slight varia-
tion to the Dual Route Resolution Framework.

Professionals are obliged to uphold their professional code of
conduct at all times. Their decisions in an ethical dilemma would
turn on whether they have the conviction to hold up the ethical
standards of their profession in the face of consequences. Such
ethical dilemmas will be discussed in Chapter 8 (Codes of Ethical
Conduct).

Application

Let us consider how the Dual Route Resolution Framework can be
applied.

Case 1 (from Chapter 1)

Jason, the CEO of the construction company, is pondering over
whether to report the two young employees for taking narcotic
drugs. One of the employees is the sole breadwinner of his family.
The ethical dilemma is Compliance with Company Policy versus
Compassion. A consequence of non-compliance would be that the
CEO is seen as not setting a good example as a leader in the organisation. On the other hand, complying with policy would cause a
family to suffer from a lack of income and create the perception of
an uncaring company in the eyes of employees.

Jason can mitigate the consequences of either decision path. If
he chooses not to report the employees, he can take stern disciplinary action against them, e.g. giving them a warning (as suggested
by his foreman) and impose a stoppage of an annual salary incre-
ment. In short, he is not allowing the two to go scot-free. The
company board would probably not disagree. If necessary, Jason can
consult with the company chairman or another board member to
get buy-in.

If Jason, instead, chooses to report the two employees, he can mitigate the suffering of the family of the sole breadwinner, e.g. by providing some form of financial assistance and even assurance of re-hiring him upon his rehabilitation.

In the end, after deliberation, Jason took the path of upholding company policy, but not for the lack of courage to breach it. It was because he has found a way to still uphold the code of morality, by mitigating the consequences through offering compassionate assistance to the affected family of one of the employees.

Case 2 (from Chapter 2)

The interrogators are considering the use of torture (a criminal offence) to extract information from the captured terrorist on the location of a planted time-bomb. The ethical dilemma is Compliance with Law versus Saving Lives. If the interrogators comply with the law and refrain from using torture, the consequences would be the likely loss of many lives and probably also a lifetime of regret. The decision turns on whether the interrogators have the conviction to take the morality route and the courage to face the consequences.

Professor Simon Chesterman who broached this scenario in his article[1] published in The Straits Times wrote that when he used this time bomb scenario in his classes to explore issues concerning the use of torture, occasionally his students would press him on what he would do if faced with such a situation. His answer was: *"There is no good answer. The least bad answer is that, if I were genuinely convinced that the threat was real, that the perpetrator was guilty, and that the method was the only one that would work, then I might well resort to torture. And then, regardless of whether I was correct in my assumptions, I should go to prison."*

---

[1] Chesterman, S. (2014, December 17). Lessons on the Use of Torture. The Straits Times. Professor Simon Chesterman is Dean and Professor of Law at the National University of Singapore.

Case 3

One of my former students has just returned from working in a third world country. Recalling one of my lectures where I touched on the subject of corruption, she asked whether it would be wrong for the mother of a girl who had been sexually assaulted to bribe the police, who would otherwise be slow to act on her police report. Under the Dual Route Resolution Framework, the principles in conflict in this ethical dilemma are Compliance with Law (do not bribe) versus Justice (for her daughter). The corresponding consequences are a lifetime of regret (for not bribing to obtain justice) and a jail term (for committing bribery). If the mother is prepared to face a jail term, she would proceed with giving the bribe. In all likelihood, given a mother's instinct to protect her child, she should have the conviction and courage to break the law to secure justice for her child. This becomes easier if corruption is a way of life in the country.

Moral Dilemmas

Moral dilemmas (as distinct from ethical dilemmas) cannot be resolved using the Dual Route Resolution Framework. Those are dilemmas where the conflict is not between a Code of Conduct and a Code of Morality, but between two Codes of Morality. Consider two scenarios:

Scenario 1

An abjectly poor family has three children; two of the children are twins and they are newborns. The family ponders how they could possibly afford to raise three children. They are considering whether to give away one of the twins for adoption. The family has to decide between keeping the family intact and its long-term well-being. The consequences of their decision would be heartbreak (adoption route) or long-term hardship and a lower quality of life for the family.

Scenario 2

The earlier case of the shipwrecked sailors (Chapter 2) can be viewed as a moral dilemma, where the decision is either upholding the sanctity of life or survival as a group. The consequences would be life-long regret (for killing an innocent person) or the likely death of a few people.

In both scenarios, the decision being made is between two moral principles, instead of between law and morality. Courage to break a law therefore, has little or no role in the resolution. A different resolution process is necessary. A possible approach is pragmatism. First, identify the interests at the core of the matter that should be upheld. Then consider which of these matters the most to the decision maker and is of overriding importance.

In the first scenario, the interests are the long-term survival of the family, the well-being of each child, and keeping the family intact. In the second scenario, the interests are respect for life and group survival. In both scenarios, the decision should turn on which interest is of overriding importance and pursuing it is therefore, the less unbearable path for the decision maker.

In the first scenario, if the long-term survival of the family and the well-being of each child are deemed more important than keeping the family intact, the family would chose the adoption path. In the second scenario, if respect for life is deemed more important than survival of the group, then the life of the cabin boy would have been spared.

Tactical Approach

If, in using the Dual Route Resolution Framework, the decision maker is unable to come to a firm decision and needs to find another way, it might be helpful to consider a tactical approach. This is discussed in the next chapter.

Summary

- For a more effective resolution, an ethical dilemma should be framed in terms of the principles in conflict, i.e. code of conduct versus code of morality.

- The Dual Route Resolution Framework provides a step-by-step procedure for decision making in an ethical dilemma. A key step is to ask yourself who you are and what you stand for.

- The decision eventually take turns on whether the decision maker has the strength of character (courage and conviction) to face the consequences.

- For a professional, his decision turns on whether he has the strength of character to uphold the code of ethical conduct, to which he has pledged, in the face of the consequences.

- The final test is whether one can sleep well with the decision taken and whether the decision can stand up to scrutiny in a public inquiry or be worthy of mention in one's eulogy.

- Resolving a "moral dilemma" (as distinct from an "ethical dilemma") requires a different approach, one that identifies the key interests at the core of the matter, and decides which of them is of overriding importance.

Questions for Reflection

1. *Think of an ethical dilemma that you have experienced or observed, e.g. in the plot of a movie. Reconstruct the ethical dilemma in the form of a Code of Conduct versus a Code of Morality decision. What are the consequences under each of the decision paths? Which path was taken?*

2. *The partners of a family business are pondering whether to terminate the service of the CEO, who is a family member. Following a whistleblower*

complaint, the CEO was found to have been siphoning off money from the business for several years. The CEO did not deny the charge, but reasoned that he had contributed to the business growth despite receiving a salary that he deemed too modest. One third of the partners want a change of CEO and the misappropriated money returned. A third disagrees for reason of kinship. The remaining third is indifferent.

If you were the chairman of the company, how would you guide the deliberation process among the partners towards an effective resolution?

6. RESOLUTION: TACTICAL APPROACH

In 1999, I watched a performance of the musical "Fiddler on the Roof"[1] staged by the Singapore Lyric Theatre.[2] The lead character in the story is a good-humoured Jewish patriarch called Teyve. There was a scene where a group of village folk were having an argument. The following exchange really amused me:

Townsperson: "Why should I break my head about the outside world? Let the outside world break its own head...."

Tevye (*pointing to the Townsperson*): "He is right..."

Perchik: "Nonsense. You can't close your eyes to what's happening in the world."

Tevye (*pointing to Perchik*): "He's right."

Rabbi's pupil: "He's right, and he's right. They can't both be right!"
Tevye (*pauses, then pointing to the Rabbi's pupil*): "You know, you are also right."

Out of diplomacy, Teyve took no sides in the argument. He didn't choose between Right and Right. But when one is dealing with an ethical dilemma, one has to make a clear decision between two decision paths.

---

[1] *Fiddler on the Roof* is a musical based on a story by Joseph Stein, set in Imperial Russia in 1905, with music by Jerry Bock and lyrics by Sheldon Harnick.
[2] The Singapore Lyric Theatre is now called the Singapore Lyric Opera.

Which decision path is "more right" is a matter of personal judgement, based on one's value system and strength of character, and by having regard for the consequences of each decision path.

In my talks on ethical dilemmas, for each case study that I presented, I would first conduct a poll to see how the participants would decide. They can choose either of two decision paths or "None of the above".

Invariably there would be a small number who would choose "None of the above". This small number of participants might have seen a way out of the dilemma, perhaps a clever compromise that avoids breaching any of the principles in conflict. Finding such a win-win solution should always be in the mind of the decision maker. It might take some effort and creativity to find such a solution.

Consultation

To begin with, resolving an ethical dilemma should not be rushed unless the circumstances require an immediate decision. It should be handled with proper and adequate consideration of the options. Doing so also enables the cooling of any emotions that might cloud one's judgement.

It might also be helpful to consult a mentor, or a trusted friend or colleague, who could provide fresh insights on the issue, and inspire you with his wisdom and experience to find your way forward.

Wait and Watch

Let us look at some examples of ethical dilemmas where a tactical approach can be found.

In the story of the 2016 high action thriller, *Eye in the Sky*,[3] mentioned in Chapter 2, a British colonel was commanding an

---

[3] Hood, G. (2015). *Eye in the Sky*. Entertainment One. *Eye in the Sky* is a film starring Helen Mirren, *et al.*, based on a story by Guy Hibbert.

operation to identify and eliminate a group of members of a terrorist cell who were congregating in a house in Nairobi to make preparations for a terror attack. Aided by aerial surveillance and a ground based stealth camera, the plan was to launch an aerial bombing attack on the house. As the operation team was about to launch the attack, a little village girl suddenly appeared. She set up a makeshift stall just outside the compound of the target to sell bread that her mother had baked. This caused an ethical dilemma for the operation team.

The colonel delayed the launch of the attack hoping that the girl would soon sell off her bread and leave the spot. As time dragged on and the operation reached a critical stage, a local undercover agent was activated to buy the last two remaining loaves of bread from the little girl to speed up her departure from the scene. This worked, but unfortunately, before the girl could move away to a safe distance, the aerial attack had to be launched.

The colonel in dealing with her ethical dilemma adopted a "wait-and-watch" approach.

In an ethical dilemma, if time permits, one should refrain from making an immediate decision, but instead monitor the situation, looking out for a window of opportunity to achieve a better outcome with fewer consequences. While doing so, one must be ever ready to make the decision quickly if the situation becomes critical and a decision must be taken.

Win-Win Resolutions

In some ethical dilemmas, there might be scope for a win-win solution where both principles in conflict can be upheld, even if only partially. Consider these examples:

Case 1

A high school requires a security deposit of $3,000 from foreign students to discourage withdrawal once the academic term has started. Under the school's policy, a refund is not allowed except when the student is leaving for health reasons. The parent of a foreign student appealed for refund of such a deposit on the ground that he was being posted by his company to another country. Under the rules, the deposit would be forfeited. While the rules were clear, it could be argued that there should be some flexibility exercised. In the end, a pragmatic solution was found. A modest discount in the refund amount was given. This upheld the spirit of the no-refund policy while showing some compassion for the student's family.

Case 2

An expatriate couple on a 3-year "teaching couple" contract with an elementary school has been receiving a *"teaching couple housing allowance"* of $3,000 per month. The school board approved a discretionary increase of 3% in housing allowances for all expatriate teachers. As the increase is discretionary, the school management denied this couple the increase as it found out that they were actually not married and it would be contrary to the school's governance rules to regard a partner as a spouse. The couple appealed to the school board for fair treatment as their job application did not require a declaration of legal marital status. The decision in the ethical dilemma is between upholding the employment contract (that provides for periodic adjustment of housing allowance) and upholding the governance rules of the school.

After careful deliberation, the board decided to give the couple the increase in housing allowance on grounds of fair treatment, but only for the remaining duration of their contract. Thereafter, the two teachers would be considered for individual single teacher contracts, should the school decide to continue employing them. This decision upholds in spirit both the moral principle of fairness and the governance rules of the school.

Case 3

A rather common ethical dilemma in administration relates to a purchase made without the requisite prior approval. For example, a photocopier was purchased at $6,000 without prior approval. The photocopier had been delivered. The executive responsible approached his manager for his retrospective approval of the purchase. However, the manager felt that the purchase was not fully justified as the photocopier purchased had unnecessary features. A simpler machine would have cost only about $4,000.

The manager was facing an ethical dilemma between giving retrospective approval to enable payment to be made to the supplier and upholding his integrity, and refusing to give the requisite approval. The consequence of the latter is that the supplier would not be paid.

At two talks, I presented this scenario to see how many participants would acquiesce thus, compromising one's integrity. The poll result averaged over the two talks is as follows:

I will give retrospective approval: 44%
I will not give retrospective approval: 30%
None of the above: 26%

44% of participants were prepared to compromise their integrity presumably so that supplier can receive his due payment. Among the participants who voted "None of the above", the one who spoke up suggested that the purchase be annulled and the photocopier returned to the supplier. I then asked: "Is that not being unfair to the supplier? There might also be a penalty for breach of contract."

A possible solution that I suggested is this: The manager should not give retrospective approval of the purchase. Instead, he should seek the approval of the appropriate higher authority (e.g. Board's finance committee) to pay the supplier to meet the contractual obligation notwithstanding that there was no approval of the purchase, citing the unusual circumstances of the case. Then the executive who is responsible for the lapse in procedure should be counseled.

Such a course of action, unorthodox as it might be, ensures that the manager's integrity is not compromised and that the supplier is paid. The counselling of the responsible executive has the salutary effect of deterring similar breaches of procedure in future.

When dealing with an ethical dilemma, one should always try to find a tactical way to deal with it so that both the Code of Conduct and the Code of Morality can be upheld, even if only partially.

Summary

- In resolving an ethical dilemma, it is helpful to consult a mentor, trusted friend or colleague who could provide fresh insights and inspire you with his wisdom and experience.

- In resolving an ethical dilemma, it might be possible to apply a tactical approach, such that both principles in conflict can be upheld, even if only partially.

- If time permits, a wait-and-watch strategy allows changing circumstances to provide a window of opportunity for a better outcome, including possible avoidance of the cause of the ethical dilemma.

Questions for Reflection

1. *Think of an ethical dilemma that you have experienced or observed. Was a tactical approach used to resolve it? If not, can you think of a tactical way to deal with it?*

2. *Kevin was hired as a "senior instructor" at $4,100 per month. He completed his probation successfully. At the end of the year, he received a*

bonus for good performance. Months later, two other senior instructors informally complained that Kevin seemed lacking ground experience for a senior instructor.

A check on Kevin's CV showed that he previously had 2 years experience as an instructor and 3 years as a training administrator. The HR Department had wrongly interpreted training administration as similar to actual training. All the other senior instructors had 5 to 8 years of actual training experience when they were hired.

Kevin should have been offered just a "trainer" position at $3,300. He is now overpaid by almost 20%. The CEO is pondering over how to deal with the situation. He is in an ethical dilemma.

What are the principles in conflict? What are the alternative courses of action and their consequences? If you were the CEO, what would you do? Is there a tactical way to deal with the ethical dilemma?

ETHICAL DILEMMAS
IN PERSPECTIVE

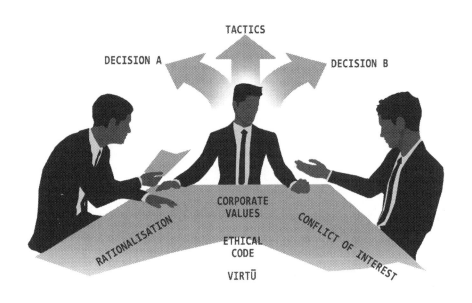

7. LIFTING A FINGER

Ten years ago, I was at a barbershop at Serangoon Gardens for a ten-dollar haircut. There was a hand-written notice taped to the payment machine indicating that it was out-of-order. At the prompting of one of the barbers, I handed to her my ten-dollar bill. No receipt was issued. While my hair was being trimmed, it dawned on me that it was the second time in about a month that the payment machine was out of order.

I became suspicious that those employees might have been stealing from the till. I thought of asking the barber who took my ten dollars why no receipt was issued, but decided that it would be more prudent if I raise my concern with the company.

The next day I telephoned the company and the owner answered. Jack was the sole-proprietor and he owned three barbershops all with similar payment machines. He told me that he had a full-time job and running the three barbershops was his sideline job. He had suspected that his employees might have been cheating him, but he had no time to conduct surprise checks. I suggested that he install a camera in all the three barbershops and also put up a permanent sign telling customers that no payment should be made to the staff.

The following month when I went for my next haircut in the same barbershop, I found that Jack had done exactly as I had suggested.

I could well have overlooked the matter and minded my own business. After all, I did get my hair trimmed and was not overcharged. But I decided that it was not right to turn a blind eye, and not lift a finger, when there was a telltale sign of criminal misappropriation happening.

Bystander Dilemma

This case illustrates what is known as "Bystander Dilemma". An observer of a wrongdoing might stand idly by and not intervene, even if he is able to. The bystander may not want to get involved for fear of a negative response or being misunderstood.

Yick K H, a long-time friend, once shared his experience with me. One day, he was having lunch at a food centre. A woman at the next table was incessantly scolding her little daughter for being slow in finishing her plate of chicken rice. The woman probably had a bad day, but the little girl looked embarrassed being scolded in a public place. My friend walked over to the woman and politely suggested that she tone down her admonishment and give the little girl a hug. Instead of calming down, the woman challenged my friend to take a video recording of her and post it on social media. Exasperated, my friend walked away. However, his message did get through as the scolding stopped and the little girl finished her plate of chicken rice in an unrushed manner.

Studies have shown that the more people there are at the scene of an emergency, the less likely a person would step forward and offer help. This phenomenon is called the "Bystander Effect".[1]

When one comes across a person in need of assistance and there is no one else around, one should not assume that the next person would provide assistance. Avoiding action in a bystander dilemma is generally not desirable as a chance is missed to bring about a moral outcome to the situation.

Workplace Bystander Dilemma

A bystander dilemma can also happen in the workplace. Employees have an obligation to apply themselves fully in their jobs. This includes actively contributing to the discussions at a meeting. It is

---

[1] Darley, J. M., & Latane, B. (1968). Bystander intervention in emergencies: Diffusion of responsibility. *Journal of Personality and Social Psychology*, 8(4, Pt.1), 377–383. https://doi.org/10.1037/h0025589.

not unusual to see a few staff members at a meeting not speaking up, perhaps out of a fear of saying something wrong. They choose to be bystanders. Often it is necessary for the chairman of a meeting to encourage staff members to share their views.

And when a staff member sees something amiss in the organisation, he should also voice his concern, but do so in an appropriate way. Consider this example.

Jane is an executive of a company. She has become aware that the CEO has not been complying with the hiring procedure. He has had a few of his colleagues from his previous company hired and appointed to senior positions without getting the requisite approval of the chairman of the human resource committee. Several other executives have also observed such irregularities in hiring practice. Jane could have looked aside and considered it as none of her business. However, as there is a whistleblowing reporting channel in the company, she decided to file an anonymous report through it.

The Powerful Bystander

There is another kind of bystander dilemma. This involves a person who has the authority to intervene in a situation. He might choose not to do so, exercising his "right of discretion". Whether a person with authority does intervene depends on how he sees his role and interprets the limits of his authority. Even if his hands are tied, it might be possible for him to apply his influence in some way to help out in a situation for moral reasons.

Consider this example. The CEO of a company has terminated the service of a manager for breaching a government tender submission procedure resulting in the company's bid for a $20 million IT contract being deemed invalid. The manager did not appeal against his dismissal. In fact, he wrote a letter of apology and accepted the dismissal.

Andrew, the company's general counsel became aware of the dismissal. After getting the facts of the case, he felt that the dismissal might not be in order because of an absence of due process. The dismissal of an employee has to be approved by the Board human resource committee.

Since the manager had accepted his dismissal, Andrew could well have just let the matter rest. However, he felt that professionally he should still provide the CEO with his views. This he did.

Consequently, the CEO, rather reluctantly, brought the case to the human resource committee for its retrospective approval of the dismissal. The committee decided that the manager should not have been summarily dismissed as the breach of tender submission procedure was his first mistake in his 5 years of service to the company. However, since the CEO had already dismissed him, as a gesture of goodwill, the departing manager was given an ex-gratia payment for his past service.

Andrew had the "right of discretion" as the matter was not brought to his attention for legal advice (the normal procedure), and also the matter was technically over since the manager had accepted his dismissal. There was therefore, little risk of a legal challenge from him. But because of his strong conviction as a professional, Andrew intervened and this resulted in a moral outcome.

Summary

- "Bystander dilemma" refers to a situation where a person witnessing a wrong doing being perpetrated is in a conundrum whether or not to intervene.

- Non-intervention may be because of fear of being misunderstood or of facing some consequences, or because there are others who can intervene.

- Avoiding action in a bystander dilemma is generally not desirable as a chance might have been missed to bring about a moral outcome to the situation.

- This is especially so in the case of a "powerful bystander", one who has the ability and authority to intervene and assist in the situation.

Question for Reflection

You are at a staff meeting when the boss starts to berate a colleague in a harsh manner for his presentation that seems poorly prepared and unhelpful. The colleague is clearly distressed and could hardly respond with a coherent explanation. Everyone else at the meeting remain silent. Despite your relatively junior rank you feel that you should not be a bystander. What can you do?

8. CODES OF ETHICAL CONDUCT

"One's fitness as a professional is inextricably linked to the ethical impera-
tives to which one is bound. For lawyers, we swear an oath upon admission
to the Bar. Similarly, the physician's pledge binds the new doctor to a
number of public-spirited commitments. "[1]

— Sundaresh Menon
Chief Justice of Singapore

The work of lawyers, doctors, accountants, auditors, engineers, social workers, etc. is governed by codes of ethical conduct laid down by the respective professional bodies. The codes set out the ethical principles and standards that the practitioners are required to uphold when they serve their clients. Typically, a code of ethical conduct of a profession covers these main areas: Integrity, Objectivity, Technical Competency, Confidentiality, and Professionalism.

Compliance with a code of ethical conduct reflects the Deontological Principle that says that the morality of an action should be based on whether it is right or wrong in itself regardless of the consequences. Hence, if an auditor compromises on his code of ethical conduct and turns a blind eye on a serious accounting lapse, that would be wrong whatever might be his own reason for doing so. He would be betraying the trust that the public has on him.

---

[1] Menon, S. (2017). 23rd Gordon Arthur Ransome Oration: Law and Medicine: Professions of Honour, Service and Excellence. Annals, Academy of Medicine Singapore, 46(9), 356–363. A speech delivered at the 23rd Gordon Arthur Ransome Oration held on 21 July 2017.

A code of ethical conduct of a profession is sacrosanct and non-negotiable. Breaching a code of ethical conduct would result in disciplinary proceedings being taken by the relevant professional body or government regulatory body.

At a talk for a group of social workers, I posed the following scenario: Rebecca, medical social worker, has been caring for a patient who was in the mental hospital for two weeks. Because of a shortage of beds, the hospital administration requires five patients to be discharged to make room for more serious cases. Rebecca's patient is one of the five patients identified.

In Rebecca's own assessment, her client is not ready for immediate discharge; he would need to stay at least two more days in the hospital. Rebecca ponders over whether she should simply accept the hospital's directive or appeal to the hospital to re-assess the patient's suitability for discharge.

I posed the question: If you were in Rebecca's shoes, what would you do? Three answer choices were given and the poll result is as follows:

Appeal to have patient remain in hospital: 57%
Accept the hospital's decision: 29%
None of the above: 14%

The majority would try to find a way to have the patient stay longer than otherwise allowed by the hospital. This reflects strong conviction in going the extra mile to uphold professional standards.

Avoiding Conflict of Interest

Professional standards can sometimes be compromised by the very nature of work arrangements. This was happening not too long ago in the field of auditing when a public accounting firm could provide paid non-audit services, e.g. consultancy services, to a company that it was auditing. This created a conflict of interest situation. The independence of the audit was compromised as the audit firm had a business interest in the company it was auditing.

Following the Enron scandal in 2001, a law was put in place in USA (the Sarbanes-Oxley Act) that, among other things, prohibits a public accounting firm from providing non-auditing services to a client whose accounts it is auditing.

But a situation of conflict of interest remains in another category of auditing, namely, "internal auditing". The duty of an internal auditor is to assist the company's board in its oversight responsibilities. The board therefore, counts on the internal auditor to be independent of the management of the company.

Although the internal audit department reports to the company's audit committee on their work, on administrative matters (such as obtaining manpower and financial resources, and even promotion and salary matters), it reports to the CEO. This creates a "conflict of roles" situation in the CEO as he is both the party who has to answer for lapses found by the internal auditor and the party who has control over the resources and even career progression of the same auditor. Consequently, the internal audit department is placed at a constant risk of being in an ethical dilemma.

At a conference for internal auditors, I presented a scenario where an internal auditor is being asked by the CEO to overlook a significant financial lapse on the basis that no fraud is involved. I asked participants how they would respond if they were the internal auditor. The poll result was as follows:

Turn down request citing the ethical code: 70%
Accommodate the request: 16%
None of the above: 14%

I had hoped that no participant would be prepared to compromise on their professional integrity by agreeing to the CEO's request, but 16% of them were. This indicates the effect of the inherent ethical dilemma in the internal audit profession.

Measures can be taken to mitigate, if not eliminate, the risk of ethical dilemmas for internal audit departments. I know of two audit committees of large companies whose chairmen, acting against the grain of conventional practice, had obtained from the company board overriding authority to determine, and approve, the resourcing of the internal audit department and the career advancement of the internal auditors. This effectively removes the inherent risk of ethical dilemmas with respect to the internal audit department. But this is not a widespread practice. I see the need for the issue of the independence of internal audit departments to be addressed at the regulatory level, especially with regard to listed companies and public interest entities.

Virtù

Virtù is not a common word. It does not have exactly the same meaning as *virtue*. Some years ago, when visiting the Grand Master's Palace in Valletta in Malta, I spotted the word "*Virtù*" in one of many wall murals, each one depicting a quality trait of the knights of Malta of medieval times.

Niccolo Machiavelli[2] theorised the concept of *Virtù* as an ethical trait of successful leaders, somewhat distinct from the trait of being virtuous or having high moral standards. *Virtù* could be interpreted as "doing right", while *virtue* refers to "doing good". *Virtù* encapsulates such qualities as authority, courage, conviction, self-assuredness, and drive. *Virtù* is thus, associated with the ethical code of professionals, as well as leaders in public life.

Members of professions should not only apply their skills with technical competence and care, but they must also have the courage to uphold their code of ethical conduct under trying circumstances. They must have *Virtù* in them.

---

[2] Niccolo Machiavelli (1460–1527) was an Italian diplomat, politician, historian, philosopher, humanist and writer during the Renaissance period.

Oath Taking

Some professions require their members to take a oath to uphold their respective codes of ethical conduct. Oath taking has a salutary effect; it is a personal declaration of commitment to uphold the ethical principles and rules of a profession, to protect the interest of the people it serves.

On completion of my engineering studies in Canada in the spring of 1974, I took an oath to abide by a code of ethics called the "Obligation of an Engineer" at a ceremony called "The Ritual of the Calling of an Engineer".[3] The wording of the oath, penned by poet Rudyard Kipling, has the following concluding paragraph:

> *"For my assured failures and derelictions, I ask pardon beforehand, of my betters and my equals in my Calling here assembled; praying that in the hour of my temptation, weakness and weariness, the memory of this my Obligation and of the company before whom it was entered into, may return to me to aid, comfort and restrain."*

An oath taking ceremony of a profession has the salutary effect of etching in the memory of a practitioner, his duty to uphold the ideals of his profession in his service to society. I remember my engineer's oath to this day even though I have long left the practice.

Summary

- The work of professionals is governed by a code of ethical conduct laid down by their respective professional bodies.

- Such codes are sacrosanct and non-negotiable and should be upheld with *Virtù*.

- Pledge taking is a declaration of commitment to uphold one's code of ethical conduct. It has salutary effects.

---

[3] The Ritual of the Calling of an Engineer is administered by The Corporation of the Seven Wardens (*Société des Sept Gardiens*).

Question for Reflection

A $1.0 million loan was given to a company. The auditor later found that based on the bank's standard credit assessment method, the loan quantum should have been $0.5 million. The cause of the lapse was a misrepresentation of the credit worthiness of the company by a loan assessment officer who is in a conflict of interest situation with regard to that loan application.

In the audit report, the heading for the lapse is "False Credit Assessment". The head of the loans division, while accepting the audit finding, asks that the word "false" be changed to "wrong" as otherwise the officer concerned would be subject to a disciplinary inquiry.

If you were the auditor, how would you respond to the request?

9. CORPORATE CORE VALUES

Look up the core values of a company where a major fraud, bribery or financial scandal has just occurred and it would not be surprising to find among them, values such as "integrity", "transparency" or "accountability". What do such core values mean in those cases? Are they just for adorning the walls of the corporate headquarters?

Core values established by a company are its message to stakeholders about how it conducts its business and management functions. Besides integrity, transparency, and accountability, other typical corporate core values include trust, commitment, customer focus, service, and excellence.

The core values of a company are akin to the code of ethical conduct for professions. They are not a string of powerful words, but a policy statement of what the company stands for. It is also a moral compass for guiding the company's response to a crisis affecting customer and investor interests.

To be effective, a company's core values must be ingrained into its organisational culture. They should be regularly articulated by the management at staff conferences or other such events. It is critical that those at senior levels of management, through their conduct at work, uphold the corporate values of the company and are seen to be dong so. All this sets the right "tone at the top".

To be truly effective, a company's core values should also be reflected in the company's management and administrative systems (e.g. internal control system and performance management system). Otherwise, it is just paying them "lip service".

Effective Core Values

Core values should be purposeful. Five elements should be present:

1. *They are explained in practical terms to employees.*
2. *They are regularly articulated by management.*
3. *They are upheld by those at senior levels to set good examples.*
4. *They are reflected in the management and administrative systems, e.g. internal controls and staff compensation system.*
5. *They are used as guides in decision-making on issues with ethical or moral implications.*

Corporate Fraud

When a company's core values are breached and fraud has occurred, e.g. tax evasion, accounting fraud or corruption, it is not a situation of code of conduct versus code of morality; it is a simultaneous breach of both codes. Hence, it is not a situation of an ethical dilemma, at least not for the mastermind in the crime.

A corporate fraud would likely involve a number of employees, each playing a different colluding role in their respective areas of work (e.g. finance and accounting, contracts, or payments). The accomplices down the line might have initially faced an ethical dilemma situation when induced to perform certain actions that is part of a larger scheme of deception. They might not have had the conviction to stand firm and not get involved. But once they have crossed the line, it would likely be difficult to get out.

Corruption

While a corporate fraud can cause massive losses of company funds, shareholder value and jobs, corruption is no less abhorrent a crime. Unlike in a fraud, for corruption, the telltale signs are more elusive in the accounts of the company involved. For the company whose employee gives a bribe, the money would likely be disguised as part of a payment to an agent or supplier under a seemingly legitimate arrangement. Ordinarily, telltale signs of corruption do not show up in a regular audit of the accounts of a company, unless there is a whistleblower who provides a lead.

While the receiver of a bribe, in exchange for awarding a contract, knows that he is cheating the company, the other company that gives the bribe would likely see it as just a cost of doing business, especially in places where corruption is a way of life.

Corruption that occurs in a public sector body results in public funds being siphoned away. In exchange for a bribe, the corrupt public officer would allow a public contract to be awarded to a supplier at an inflated price.

If unchecked, corruption can easily become a way of life, not just a fact of life, in a country. Ordinary citizens suffer as the country, having been over paying on public projects because of bribes received, has less public funds for infrastructure development and social services. This is why corruption is regarded as a bane of society, the law on corruption typically prescribes very heavy penalties for those found guilty of giving or receiving bribes. The company concerned would also be penalised through a heavy fine and suffer a loss of reputation.

It is not uncommon to hear some people in business and industry lamenting that it would be extremely difficult to do business in some countries without being able to make "business facilitation payments" from time to time. There will be no end to such argument or rationalisation. At the end of the day, it is for the business executive in such a situation to make his decision, knowing the consequences that will befall his company and himself when the bribery comes to light.

Conflict of Interest

An ethical dilemma at a workplace can arise from a conflict of interest situation, for example, when a member of a committee making an investment or procurement decision has a pecuniary interest in a party that can potentially benefit from the decision. Companies with good corporate governance practices would have a policy requiring employees, as well as board members, to declare any conflict of interest in a decision-making process and to recuse himself from any involvement in the process.

However, there is another kind of conflict of interest situation where there is a secondary effect that lingers even after the conflicted party has recused himself from the decision-making. Called a "conflict of role", an example is when two employees of a company are related and one of them is in a job that reports to the other. In such a situation, the normal remedy is have the more junior employee report to a higher level executive. This is not ideal from a performance management perspective. But there is still the risk that the assigned supervisor cannot be completely objective in his assessment of performance because of the relationship. In some companies, employees are required by policy to declare any relationship with another employee in the company. Related employees are not allowed to work in the same department and one might be posted to a subsidiary company.

Whistleblowing Policy

Most companies, especially listed companies, have a whistleblowing channel for the reporting of suspicious unethical activities occurring in the company. Such a policy is an instrument of the company's board for the exercise of its oversight responsibilities.

Having a whistleblowing policy spares an employee from being in an ethical dilemma when he observes any wrongdoing or misconduct, especially one that occurs at a senior level in the company. It provides a safe avenue for reporting without a fear of reprisal.

Typical wrongdoings that come under a whistleblowing policy include fraud, criminal misappropriation, criminal breach of trust, theft, abuse of authority, breach of financial rules, staff harassment or intimidation, and any act that may cause reputation damage to the company.

Summary

- The core values of a corporation represent a policy statement on the values and principles that the company pledges to uphold in its business and management practices.

- Typical core values of a company are integrity, transparency, accountability, trust, commitment, customer focus, service, and excellence.

- Core values are the moral compass that guides a company in its conduct of business, including decision-making on matters with moral implications.

- Core values should be reflected in the management and administrative system of the company, e.g. its internal control system and staff compensation system.

- Core values are effective only if they are regularly articulated and their compliance is taken into account in staff benefits and reward systems.

- There must be a "tone at the top" to ensure that the core values are understood and internalised by all employees.

(Continued)

(Continued)

- Conflict of interest is a common cause of ethical dilemmas. An employee, or board member in a conflict of interest should declare his interest and recuse himself from any involvement in the decision-making process.

- Conflict of role is a category of conflict of interest where there is a secondary effect that lingers even after the conflicted party has recused himself from the work activity concerned.

- A whistleblowing policy, by providing an anonymous reporting channel, spares an employee of an ethical dilemma; it enables him to report suspicion of wrongdoing in the company without fear of reprisal.

Questions for Reflection

1. *A man sent his car for repair as its electronic alert system was giving false alarms under a certain condition. The car company found that the software could not be fixed because of an inherent problem in the software code. The only solution is to replace the software with the latest version. The cost is $1,800. The customer asked why repair was not possible. Should the car company tell the truth, i.e. that there is an inherent flaw in the software code? How would you handle the matter?*

2. *The Chief Operating Officer has to make a decision in a particularly challenging ethical dilemma with serious consequences for the company. He forms a committee comprising the various heads of department to consider the consequences and to provide him with views and recommendations. What are your views on this approach?*

10. WITHOUT FEAR OR FAVOUR

In 1975, soon after joining the Singapore government service as a public works engineer, I underwent a two-week induction course at the Civil Service Staff Development Institute.[1]

My most vivid recollection of the course was a session on its last day. The trainer was gentleman from Canada by the name of John Chen and he wore cowboy boots. He presented a laundry list of "dos and don'ts" for civil servants that was intended to be read in reverse. For example: *"DO: If you have savings in your budget, do try to spend it all."* and *"DON'T: If your assignment is difficult, don't work overtime to complete it."* Who can forget such avant-garde advice to rookie public officers?

What struck me even more was a poignant advice that John shared: *"A good civil servant is one who is prepared to quit."* It was a rather disconcerting message for officers who had just embarked on their public service career.

The message was that a public officer should carry out his duties to the people and country with integrity or, to use a cliché, "without fear or favour", which means "with fairness and impartiality". The phrase also implies having the courage to do the right thing when serving the public interest.

Courage to Speak Up

Courage should also be manifested in how a public officer conducts himself at his workplace. I had often encouraged my officers to

---

[1] The institute is now called the Civil Service College.

71

speak up at meetings and not be a bystander. I know that they have views or ideas to share, but might have trepidation in proactively speaking up for fear of saying the wrong thing or being misunderstood. In 2015, soon after I retired from public service, the public service newsletter, "Challenge Magazine", invited me to write an article on speaking up in the form of a "Letter to A Young Officer". The article is reproduced in the Annex of this book.

Ethical Dilemmas in Public Service

Government and public service work is not without ethical dilemmas. These can occur at two levels. The first is policy level. When there are morality implications in a new policy being contemplated or formulated, public consultation is essential. For example, in 2004, the Singapore government considered departing from its long held policy of not allowing casinos in the country. There was intense public debate on the matter. Following months of public discourse on various platforms, Parliament approved the proposal of having "integrated resorts" with casinos.

At the operational level, ethical dilemmas that arise are resolved by the department concerned or the officers exercising authority. What guides the decision-making is a desire to achieve the best outcome for a member of the public in need, withing the overall policy framework.

Here is an example from my own experience: At a citizenship appeals committee session, when a certain case was being considered, an officer cautioned that a decision to allow the appeal might set a precedent as there were several somewhat similar cases. The committee chairman had a different view. He said: "There is no such thing as a precedent. No two cases are identical. Each must be considered on its own merit." That articulation was a helpful lesson for decision-making in the public interest. It enabled us to make courageous and moral decisions without fear of creating a precedent.

Courage to Look Beyond a Rule

In a bureaucracy, decisions and actions are generally rule-based. This ensures fairness in terms of consistency of service delivery and decision-making. However, when applied in an unthinking manner, the outcome might not be optimal or even desirable.

An applicant for a grant missed the grant submission deadline. He appealed for special consideration explaining why he could not wait for the next application cycle. The officer concerned would have generally taken a "rule-based" approach and rejected the application. This is to be fair to all. It would be ideal if public officers are given greater leeway to interpret rules when dealing with cases that "fall in between the cracks". This would enable them to make more helpful or moral decisions when serving the public interest.

Public officers should also not be afraid to look beyond a rule and act in a manner that upholds morality, so long as the policy or principle behind it is upheld.

In the 1990s, when I was working as an Administrative Service officer in a ministry, a human resource manager came to me for advice. A number of staff members had been selected for a customised diploma course to upgrade their competencies as manager level social work officers. A few of them were having difficulty finding a "surety" for the required undertaking that, on completion of the course, they would remain in service for a specified minimum period. This was a standard rule applied across the public service.

I was somewhat in an ethical dilemma. While the rule was clear, I could also see the awkwardness, and even embarrassment, that those officers (some in their 40s) would feel if they have to ask a relative or friend to be a guarantor to pay for the cost incurred by the ministry if he were to abscond after completing the course.

After some consideration, I decided not to apply the rule in this particular instance. The human resource manager was aghast with my decision as a public service rule was being breached. I explained to her that it was unlikely that a long serving officer would uproot and leave the country after getting the diploma. Therefore, the officer's signature alone in his letter of undertaking should suffice for its enforcement. The principle behind the rule requiring a surety would be substantially upheld.

Rules *vis-à-vis* Principles

Because a rule cannot cover all circumstances, one may sometimes need to fall back on its underlying principle to guide one's actions. Following a rule in an unthinking manner may bring about unintended consequences. In fact, it might even result in a breach of the very principle behind it, and this would be worse.

Consider this case. In the late 1970's, at a financial management course that I was attending as a young officer, the then Auditor-General, Mr Chee Keng Soon, shared this anecdote about wastage of public funds arising from the blind compliance with rules, as reported in the Report of the Auditor-General.[2] A deckhand of the Customs & Excise Department was over-paid a day's wage of $8.15 when he vacated office. Pursuant to the relevant rules, efforts were made to recover the money. As the former deckhand was living on a rural island, three round trips were made using a speedboat of the department in the recovery efforts. This resulted in about $300 worth of petrol being consumed. In complying with the rules regarding recovery of losses, the larger principle of minimising loss or wastage had taken a back seat. Prudence should have been exercised and the small amount owed written off after the first unsuccessful recovery attempt.

Ironically, in another audit report thirty years later, in 2007, the writing-off of uncollected money was deemed a lapse. The case[3] involved $3.4 million in unpaid library fines that the National

---

[2] Chee, K. S. (1977). Report of the Auditor-General for the Financial Year 1976/77, p. 23. Republic of Singapore, Auditor-General Office.

[3] Lim, S. P. (2007). Report of the Auditor-General for the Financial Year 2006/07, p. 26. Singapore: Republic of Singapore, Auditor-General's Office.

Library Board had written off. While the procedural rules for the write-off had been complied with, the principle of due diligence was not adequately upheld in the fines collection efforts in the first instance. Following the audit report, an exercise was conducted by the National Library Board to recover the unpaid fines from the library users. Within the first four weeks of the exercise, more than $0.5 million were recovered.

It is important to remember that rules should not be blindly followed and that the principle behind a rule should always be upheld. This would lead to better decision-making in serving the public interest.

Summary

- "Without fear or favour" means acting with fairness and impartiality. It also implies the exercise of moral courage when performing one's duty.

- In an organisation, it is important that one proactively speaks up, thereby contributing to more effective discourse and decision-making. It takes some courage to not be a bystander at a meeting, especially for young officers.

- A rule should not be blindly followed. The principle behind it must not be breached.

Question for Reflection

In public service, it is fundamentally important that government departments have the trust of citizens that they would act fairly and impartially.

What are the corporate values of the public service that, if meticulously upheld, would engender public trust?

CONCLUSION

11. SEVEN RULES FOR DECISION-MAKING

In this book, I began the discussion on moral reasoning with the well-known thought experiment of a runaway trolley. The ethical dilemma posed is a monumentally troubling one because whichever way the trolley operator decides (to switch track or not to switch track), one or more innocent lives would be lost.

Fortunately, we do not live in a "trolley world". Nonetheless, some of the ethical dilemmas that one might be caught in, whether in personal or work life, can be very troubling because of the consequences that one has to face and deal with.

In an ethical dilemma, there is no unambiguously correct decision path; it is essentially about making a Right versus Right decision. Which way one chooses depends principally on where one's moral conviction lies and the strength of one's character to act on that conviction. It takes courage, as well as fortitude, to transgress a law or policy to uphold a moral code. How a person decides in an ethical dilemma speaks of who he really is. It determines how he will be remembered.

Inconvenient Questions

I will end this book by discussing a very common type of ethical dilemma that we all face from time to time in our personal or work life.

In 2009, in my annual report as Auditor-General, I emphasised the importance of "approving officers" exercising rigour in their scrutiny of spending proposals. They need to ask "*pertinent, if inconvenient, questions*".[1] As these would be questions asked by a person with authority, they typically elicit truthful answers.

In the reverse situation where a person with authority is the one facing an inconvenient question, an immediate or direct truthful answer might be elusive. That person with authority might not find it prudent to respond by telling the simple truth or to commit to a position on the matter at hand. Consider these two cases:

Case 1

A man is being asked by his six-year old granddaughter: "*Grandpa, I saw a man smoking outside the house. Was that you? Smoking is bad for health, Grandpa.*" The man is stumped by what the little girl said. He has been a discrete smoker and did not expect his granddaughter to be so perceptive. How should he respond to the little girl?

Case 2

ABC Corporation had earned a huge profit in the financial year that just ended. It's board approved a recommendation to give a one-time group performance bonus to all employees. The bonus approved is equal to a month of salary for all employees except those of director level and above; the latter would get a bonus of 1.5 months "in recognition of their rank seniority".

At a staff conference held three months later, an employee stood up at a dialogue-with-management session and made the following comment: "*I thank the Management for the one-time group bonus. But I need some enlightenment here. I note that employees who are directors and above are getting the bonus at a higher rate. Since it is for group performance, shouldn't the rate be the same regardless of position?*"

---

[1] Lim, S. P. (2009). Report of the Auditor-General for the Financial Year 2008/09, p. 3. Singapore: Republic of Singapore, Auditor-General Office.

She continued: *"Even with the same rate, the "dollar" amount that a director gets is already higher. And if any of them had performed very well, they would be separately rewarded under the individual performance bonus system.*

One of our corporate values is Teamwork. If we work hard as a team, should we not be rewarded as a team when it comes to the group performance bonus? Can Management therefore, please share with us why there is a differentiation in group performance bonus rates?"

The CEO is unprepared for such an incisive question. He is unsure about how to respond. To agree with the employee would be a tacit admission of an error in having differentiated performance bonus rates. On the other hand, the CEO also cannot disagree outright with the employee. To do so may be seen as being high-handed.

How would you respond in each of the two scenarios? The grandfather case is perhaps more straightforward. He must not lie to his granddaughter; he should simply admit that he was the person smoking, and then promise the little girl that he would quit smoking!

As for the other case, the CEO can adopt one of the following responses:

• Being open minded

Seeing that the employee may as well have pointed out an error in the performance bonus policy, it may not be prudent for the CEO to be openly engaged in a discussion on the matter. The CEO, instead, can show that he is open-minded and respond that the employee's views are worth considering and would be taken into account in the next group performance bonus pay-out.

• Rationalisation

The CEO may contrive an explanation, one that does not address the essence of the question. For example, he may respond by saying that the higher bonus rate is given in recognition of the "leadership role" of employees in higher positions. This would be a rationalisation as it is at odds with logic. The leadership responsibilities in those senior level jobs would already have been taken into account in the higher salaries of those positions.

- ### Side-stepping

The CEO may skirt the question by addressing only a peripheral aspect of it. Or, he may talk about the matter in broad or vague terms, giving the illusion of a full response. For example, he might, after thanking the employee for his comments, say that "*the feedback is appreciated and that the company would continue to take all views into account in rewarding employees as and when it is doing better than expected*".

When a person in a position of authority is faced with an inconvenient question, Trust and Respect are key factors in how he responds. What answer can one give that would engender trust and respect?

For Case 2, it would be wise for the CEO to adopt the open-minded answer and promise to take the employee's views into account for future group performance pay outs. The other two forms of reply (rationalisation and side-stepping) reflect an avoidance of responsibility. They do not help one to win trust and respect.

Seven Rules for Decision-Making

When faced with an inconvenient question, one should answer it with sincerity. In general, when a person with authority deals with any matter that has consequences on others, he has both the legal and moral duty to act in their best interest. I propose the following seven rules for responsible decision-making by a person exercising authority:

Rule 1: Know who you are

When we make a decision in the exercise of authority, we have a duty to act in the best interest of the stakeholders. We are expected to perform our role with honour and integrity, upholding the dignity of our office.

Rule 2: Listen to diverse views for better decision-making

We all have knowledge gaps and blind spots. We make better decisions when we consider the views of others before making up our mind.

Rule 3: Ensure that your decision has a moral basis

The morality of a policy or rule lies in its application. A policy or rule should not be applied perfunctorily, but with due consideration of the morality aspects of the application of the policy or rule. The pertinent moral values include fairness, empathy, and respect.

Rule 4: Be transparent

We are personally accountable for our decisions. Transparency is essential for accountability. We should be as transparent as possible with the basis of our decisions. This helps to engender trust and respect.

Rule 5: Do not rationalise

The argument for a decision made should squarely address the issue at hand. To use a seemingly logical or rational argument, but one that is actually irrelevant or peripheral, is to side-step the issue. Such argument, or "rationalisation", serves only to make one feel better after deciding not to address the matter head-on. Consequently, the issue remains effectively unresolved.

Rule 6: Do not be a bystander

We should be proactive in exercising our authority. We should not be a bystander in a situation where our authority or influence can help put things right. To remain a bystander is itself a decision.

Rule 7: Check your decision

After you have made your decision, but before its execution, reflect on whether it can stand up to scrutiny in an independent inquiry. If yes, proceed. Otherwise, review your decision.

Summary

- Life can be full of ethical dilemmas. One should have courage and conviction to make good moral decisions.

- The decision that we make in an ethical dilemma reflects who we really are, and determines how we will be remembered.

- Faced with an inconvenient question, trust and respect are the key factors a person of authority should consider. Will his answer win trust and engender respect?

- When a person with authority deals with a matter that has consequences on others, he has both a legal and moral duty to act in their best interest.

- A person in a position of authority should act in a moral and selfless manner. In this regard, a set of seven rules for decision-making is provided.

ANNEX: LETTER TO
A YOUNG OFFICER[1]

SPEAK UP. IT'S YOUR DUTY

Dear Young Officer,

It was a Saturday morning in 1989 when I had my first meeting with Professor S Jayakumar,[2] the then Minister for Home Affairs, and the ministry's senior management. I was in my first posting after joining the Administrative Service mid-career.

The Minister turned to me and asked for my comment on an immigration issue. I gave my view but with the caveat that I was just one week old in the ministry. The Minister responded: "Precisely, because you are new, you may well have the best view."

It was a lesson for me on the importance of listening to all views, and of encouraging officers to speak up, as speaking up does not come naturally to most of us.

In the 1970s, an articulate colleague had taunted me: "Why are you always so quiet?" That proved a turning point; I was determined that I would change.

---

[1] Article in Challenge Magazine, Sep/Oct 2015 issue, page 27. Re-printed with the permission of Public Service Division, Prime Minister's Office.
[2] Professor S Jayakumar was Minister for Home Affairs of Singapore from 1988 to 1994. He was Minister for Foreign Affairs of Singapore from 1994 to 2004. From 2004 until 2009, he was Deputy Prime Minister of Singapore.

Over the years, I made it a point to try to speak up. I started with small or casual meetings that were less intimidating. I also found it helpful to be thoroughly familiar with the issues to be discussed and jotted down points that I could make at meetings. In short, speaking up requires both practice and preparation.

Public officers in general do want to share their views and ideas. But I have observed that it is usually the same few officers who would speak up. The rest would remain quiet, perhaps out of fear that what they say may be deemed wrong or even silly. But why must that be so?

There is no such thing as a wrong view. A view expressed is based on your perspectives of the issue at hand and those, in turn, depend on your own knowledge, life and work experiences, and value system. In encouraging my SMU students to speak up, I use the analogy of two passengers sitting on different sides in a bus. Looking out of the windows on their side, each would invariably have a different perspective of the same scenery. Can either of them say that the other view is wrong?

In my previous work, I had encountered differing views on various issues such as the penalties and rehabilitation programmes for drug abuse. The diversity of perspectives makes for a more thorough discussion, thereby leading to better decision-making.

Once, I expressed reservation about a proposal to set up a company to promote young artists' works. I felt that its business model was not sustainable. Despite being the lone voice, my view had an effect: it was eventually decided that the proposal would not proceed until a better business model was found.

One should not refrain from contributing an idea or suggestion that is radically different. If everybody agrees with your idea, it is at best a good idea. But if most people sneer at it, you may well have hit on an innovative idea that challenges conventional wisdom.

One should also not hold back giving general comments on matters outside one's area of expertise. At a technical discussion between Minister Jayakumar and the ministry's legal officer on matters of law in anti-narcotics legislation, I could only chip in at one point. When I did so, the Minister told the legal officer: "Listen carefully. Here is a non-lawyer speaking." I was glad that my input from a layman perspective was brought to bear on the discussion.

If you are chairing a meeting or discussion, actively encourage the sharing of views and ideas. You will be amazed at how the collective wisdom of your colleagues can help achieve a better discussion outcome. But be slow in giving your own comments. I once attended a meeting where, immediately after a paper was presented, the chairman summarily said he disagreed with it. No one spoke up after that!

If the participants are still reticent, a more affirmative action can be taken. I was having afternoon tea with my wife at a cafe in Chinatown when the owner conducted an impromptu meeting with her employees. Before closing the meeting, she asked each employee, in Mandarin: "Do you have anything to raise?" She was nudging them to speak up and it worked; an employee who was hitherto silent spoke up.

I would encourage all public officers to see it as part of their job responsibility to participate actively at meetings and discussions.

Do so spontaneously. Do not wait to be asked.

Speak up, speak up and speak up!

Yours Sincerely,
Lim Soo Ping

Printed in the United States
By Bookmasters